CATS

BY ALEXIS BURLING

Essential Library

An Imprint of Abdo Publishing
abdobooks.com

ABDOBOOKS.COM

Published by Abdo Publishing, a division of ABDO, PO Box 398166, Minneapolis, Minnesota 55439. Copyright © 2024 by Abdo Consulting Group, Inc. International copyrights reserved in all countries. No part of this book may be reproduced in any form without written permission from the publisher. Essential Library™ is a trademark and logo of Abdo Publishing.

Printed in the United States of America, North Mankato, Minnesota.
052023
092023

Cover Photos: Eric Isselee/Shutterstock Images; Nynke van Holten/Shutterstock Images (back)
Interior Photos: Vladyslav Starozhylov/Shutterstock Images, 1; Eric Isselee/ Shutterstock Images, 3, 6, 16–17, 26, 74, 82, 100, 101; Elena Rozhenok/Shutterstock Images, 4–5; Andrey Kuzmin/Shutterstock Images, 7; Shutterstock Images, 11, 20, 28, 38–39, 45, 49, 57, 61, 85, 94, 97, 98; Alena Ozerova/Shutterstock Images, 13; Yakobchuk Viacheslav/Shutterstock Images, 14; DEA/G. Dagli Orti/De Agostini/Getty Images, 22; Toru Yamanaka/AFP/Getty Images, 24; Ambartsumian Valery/Shutterstock Images, 32; Craig Hudson/The Charleston Gazette-Mail/AP Images, 34; Konrad Mostert/ Shutterstock Images, 37; Tanya Dol/Shutterstock Images, 42; Jeanette Virginia Goh/ Shutterstock Images, 46; Mindy Christakes, 51; Mireya Acierto/FilmMagic/Getty Images, 52; Walt Mancini/MediaNews Group/Pasadena Star-News/Getty Images, 55; Neilson Barnard/Getty Images Entertainment/Getty Images, 63; Amerigo Images/ Shutterstock Images, 64; Singing Media/Shutterstock Images, 68; Yuriy German/ Shutterstock Images, 70; Arif Hudaverdi Yaman/Anadolu Agency/Getty Images, 71; Kathy Willens/AP Images, 76; Carlos Avila Gonzalez/San Francisco Chronicle/Hearst Newspapers/Getty Images, 78; Aleksey Mnogosmyslov/Shutterstock Images, 81; MTS Photo/Shutterstock Images, 86; Svetlana Rey/Shutterstock Images, 89; Nynke van Holten/Shutterstock Images, 90

Editor: Marie Pearson
Series Designer: Becky Daum

Library of Congress Control Number: 2022948876

PUBLISHER'S CATALOGING-IN-PUBLICATION DATA
Names: Burling, Alexis, author.
Title: Cats / by Alexis Burling
Description: Minneapolis, Minnesota: Abdo Publishing Company, 2024 | Series: Essential pets | Includes online resources and index.
Identifiers: ISBN 9781098290528 (lib. bdg.) | ISBN 9781098276706 (ebook)
Subjects: LCSH: Pets--Juvenile literature. | Cat, Domestic--Juvenile literature. | Cats--Juvenile literature. | Pets--Behavior--Juvenile literature. | Zoology--Juvenile literature.
Classification: DDC 636.0887--dc23

CONTENTS

SIAMESE

Siamese are one of the oldest breeds of domestic cats. Some of the earliest Siamese lived around palaces and temples in Siam, which is now Thailand. They were seen as the ideal breed for members of the royal family and religious scholars because of their bright blue eyes and sleek, short-haired coats. Back then, many people believed the cats were the reincarnation of souls on their journey to the afterlife.

Today, Siamese come in many forms. They are born white or ivory-colored and later develop darker sections on their ears, face, legs, and tails. Called points, these areas can be one of several colors, including dark brown (seal point), blue gray (blue point), chocolate brown (chocolate point), pinkish gray (lilac point), or reddish orange (red point).

Out of all domestic cat breeds,

Siamese have a reputation for being one of the most intelligent, curious, and talkative. They can learn tricks, open cabinets, and even turn on faucets. They can live to be anywhere from 12 to 20 years old.[1]

CHAPTER 1

CITY CAT, COUNTRY CAT

When Candi moved to the Washington countryside from urban Portland, Oregon, she was a little nervous about the move. She already loved listening to the melodious chirping of the chickadees and warblers first thing in the morning, gazing at the star-filled sky at night, and taking long walks in the hills in the late afternoon. But she worried about how her six-year-old blue point Siamese cat, Suki, would adjust.

Ever since Candi and her family arrived in their new home, Suki was acting strangely. Cats are known to take anywhere from a few days to a few weeks to adjust to new surroundings, depending on how old they are, and Suki's behavior was

Because cats are territorial, they often find it stressful to leave their home and adjust to a new one.

no different. First, she hid under the bed in Candi's room. Then, when she migrated to Candi's closet after a few days, she wouldn't come out again, even to eat. One morning, she hissed at Candi when Candi tried to pick her up to take her on a tour of the house—something Suki had never done in the past. Candi called Suki's former veterinarian to see if there were any steps she could take to help Suki feel more comfortable.

Scared cats may hide in places where they feel less likely to be threatened.

"I just don't know what to do about Suki," Candi said to the vet. "How can I help her feel at home? When she's upset, I can't relax either!"

The vet had three pieces of advice. First, Dr. Clause suggested that Candi should confine Suki to one room with her food, water, and litter box for the time being. This would help Suki feel safe and learn to trust her new surroundings. Next, the vet told Candi to create a soft and cozy rest area for Suki within that room, complete with all of her beloved toys. This would provide consistency and reassure Suki that the space was hers to explore when she was ready. Finally, Dr. Clause gave Candi a few signs to look for that would show Suki felt stressed. If Suki started overgrooming herself, pulling out her hair, peeing outside the litter box, or growling and hissing when she normally wouldn't, Candi would know to pay even more attention to Suki's needs to help calm her down.

Candi followed the vet's advice, and after nearly two weeks, Suki slowly came out of her shell. She ventured outside the closet and sniffed and rubbed her face on every surface to mark her territory with her scent. When Suki seemed curious about exploring a different room, Candi happily obliged. Candi even moved Suki's litter box into the bathroom and introduced Suki to its new permanent location. After just a day, Suki was using the litter box without any trouble.

But even though Suki seemed to finally be adapting to her new situation, Candi was still worried about one more major change. In Oregon, Suki lived almost exclusively as an indoor cat and never went outside unless in an enclosed space and under strict supervision. But in Washington, Suki wasn't alone. She was living alongside a new member of Candi's family—an outdoor tabby cat that already lived on the property when Candi and her family moved in. The previous owners couldn't take him when they moved, so Candi's parents agreed to continue his care. His name was Lady Bird, or LB for short.

A FETCHING PERSONALITY

Lots of dogs bring back a ball if it's thrown across the room. Some dogs, like the golden retriever, were even bred to retrieve. Some breeds of cats like to fetch also, including the Siamese, Chartreux, Abyssinian, and Manx. In their natural state, "cats are actually probably more prone to fetching things, and bringing things to you, than dogs," says Dr. Andrea Tu, medical director at Behavior Vets in New York City.[2] In the wild, bringing things back to the den is natural behavior for cats, she says.

INTRODUCING THE CATS

After three weeks, Suki had finally grown completely comfortable in her new home. She ate her scoop of dry food in the morning and finished the half-can of wet food Candi fed her at dinnertime. When Candi tried to get her to play fetch, Suki happily joined in on the fun. She even resumed her practice of snuggling under Candi's arm every night to help Candi go to sleep. But Candi was worried about introducing Suki to another cat.

Once again, Candi called the vet to get some advice. Dr. Clause reassured her that both cats would be fine but that Candi would need to introduce them slowly because cats are naturally territorial. Rushing the meet and greet could sabotage a positive connection that might otherwise develop naturally over time. Suki was a mostly indoor cat, and LB lived outside, so the cats wouldn't feel the need to fight over territory. Still, Candi needed to take precautions to make sure the process went smoothly.

The first step was to introduce each cat to the other's scent. Exchanging scents gives each cat important information about the other cat. It also helps both cats feel less stressed about the other's nearness. Candi spent the next week allowing Suki and LB to sniff and eventually snuggle with blankets and toys that were saturated in the other cat's scent.

When both cats seemed comfortable with the idea of another cat in the area, Candi put the next phase of the vet's plan in action. She allowed each cat to be within sight of the other, though on separate sides of a glass door. Suki stayed inside the kitchen, and LB sat on the deck on the other side of the door.

It's important to introduce cats slowly. Although some will eventually learn to get along, a bad first meeting can sour the relationship long term.

"Suki, this is LB. He lives outside and is very excited to be your friend," Candi said. "LB, this is Suki. She's a little less adventurous and shyer than you, so be gentle." Candi watched them closely.

At first, both cats showed signs of stress after seeing each other. Male cats tend to be more territorial, and LB seemed like he wanted to prove his worth. He rolled around on the deck and showed his belly. He shook his head, paced back and forth, then put his paws on the glass door, arched his back, and meowed. Suki just backed away from the window slowly, growled softly, and puffed her tail—sure signs of discomfort. Candi whisked Suki out of the room and gave her a tasty treat in the closet.

A BREAKTHROUGH

Candi was worried the cats would never get comfortable with each other. But after a few weeks of giving them treats when an interaction went smoothly, both Suki and LB seemed to be more curious than fearful. It was time to start part three of the vet's plan: physical contact.

Candi's family had a fenced-in garden on the property. Dr. Clause suggested this was the perfect place to try out the cats' first meeting. Suki would be on one side of the fence. LB would be on the other.

IN-HOME INTRODUCTIONS

Introducing a new cat to a place where another cat already lives is not only doable but it could also be the start of lifelong feline companionship. Still, owners should keep a few things in mind when introducing two indoor cats. Cat trainers advise owners to use a gate or visual barrier between the cats when introducing them for the first time. Their feeding area and litter boxes should be kept separate so the cats don't feel like someone else is taking over their territory. If a fight ever breaks out, the owner should drape a blanket over one of the cats and take them out of the room to defuse any tension.

"All right, you two, what do you think?" Candi asked the cats as she set Suki down in the enclosure. "LB, don't get too crazy! Suki, it's OK, LB's just trying to impress you. You're going to love each other in no time!"

The first interaction seemed to upset the cats. LB scampered around the yard, climbed up and down a nearby tree, and meowed constantly. Suki puffed up her tail at first, then hid behind Candi's legs. But she did rub her face against the towel with LB's scent before lying down in the grass to watch LB's antics.

After a few weeks following the same routine, the cats grew comfortable with each other's presence. Some days, they even sat by each other on either side of the

Some cats learn to enjoy the company of other cats.

Studies have shown that cat owners look more calm and even make fewer errors when their cats are present.

garden fence. Because Suki was always going to be a mostly indoor cat and LB lived outside in the barn, Candi knew they wouldn't encroach on each other's territory. She was just happy her two furry friends could live at the same home in harmony.

THE PURRFECT COMPANIONS

The American Veterinary Medical Association (AVMA) estimates nearly 62 million domestic cats live in the

United States. About 26 percent of US households have a pet cat.[3] Globally, there are more than 70 breeds of cats.[4] Since ancient times, domestic cats have provided companionship and comfort to millions of people.

Compared with more high-maintenance pets like dogs or parrots, cats are fairly easy to care for. They are intelligent and relatively self-sufficient. As predators, they can even help solve an unwanted rodent problem in the home. Controversies exist surrounding the adoption and care of domestic cats—irresponsible breeders, an out-of-control stray and feral cat population, and declawing are three of the major issues a potential owner might run into. Still, if done responsibly, research has shown that owning a cat can be one of the most rewarding experiences there is.

CHAPTER 2

THE HISTORY OF DOMESTIC CATS

All over the world, cats are viewed as a terrific pet choice. They're adorably cute. Most are friendly. They have a reputation for being one of the cleanest pets. But cats haven't always been domestic in the way they are today. Before they made themselves comfortable on couches and windowsills in homes across the world, cats big and small lived in the wild. Many still do.

Approximately 40 species of wild cats live in the world today.[1] These include everything from the reclusive bay cat of the island of Borneo to large, powerful lions and tigers. All cats are from the Felidae family, which is split into two subgroups, Pantherinae and Felinae.

When people think of wild felines, many first picture big cats like tigers.

The Pantherinae subgroup has seven cats that are mostly large. They are the tiger, lion, jaguar, leopard, snow leopard, clouded leopard, and Sunda clouded leopard. The tiger (*Panthera tigris*) is the largest of all living cats.

The Felinae subgroup contains the 33 smaller cats. They make up the majority of wild cats and are native to every continent except Antarctica and Australia. One species, the caracal, lives in Africa, the Middle East, Central Asia, and India. It gets its name from its black ears topped with tufts of fur—*caracal* means "black ears" in Turkish. The caracal can jump 10 feet (3 m) into the air to catch its prey.[2] The domestic cat also belongs in the Felinae subgroup.

All cats, wild or domestic, descended from a common ancestor, so they have several things in common. Cats are predatory animals and eat meat. Cats are also territorial. They mark the area in which they

THE FIRST WILD CAT

Scientists aren't certain when the first wild cat appeared on the planet. But many estimate that it happened between 20 and 30 million years ago. Fossil records show that the first cat was moderate in size and had retractable claws to climb up trees. It resembled a mongoose. In 1879, French naturalist Henri Filhol named this creature *Proailurus*, which means "first cat." The next set of fossils dates back 20 million years ago to a creature scientists call *Pseudaelurus*. This lynx-sized feline had a longer spine and more teeth than today's cats have.

live by rubbing their bodies on surfaces and leaving their scent. The majority of cats are solitary creatures. Aside from lions, which live in groups, most cats go about their daily lives alone.

THE DOMESTIC CAT'S EARLY ANCESTORS

Cats have lived on the planet for millions of years. But only relatively recently did the histories of cats and humans intertwine. DNA studies suggest that cats and humans lived near each other for thousands of years before cats were domesticated.

Scientists don't know exactly when humans and cats first came into contact with each other. But research suggests that wildcats called *Felis silvestris lybica*, commonly known as African wildcats, were likely first sniffing around agricultural communities in the Fertile Crescent between 8,000 and 12,000 years ago. The Fertile Crescent is a lush region in the Middle East that was home to some of the earliest human civilizations. The cats were drawn to the area because of all the rodents and other small scavengers that ate the grain and other crops stored in the farming villages. The villagers killed any larger beasts roaming through the area for food or pelts, but they left the smaller cats alone because the cats killed and ate the crop-destroying rodents.

The African wildcat weighs 7.7 to 11 pounds (3.5–5 kg).

Beginning around 1500 BCE, cat domestication sped up in Egypt and eventually spread around the world. Scientists think that humans took the cats along land and sea trade routes when they moved to new locations to help with rodent control. The more vermin the cats killed, the more the humans liked the cats and kept them around. "We think what happened is that the cats sort of domesticated themselves," says scientist Carlos Driscoll.[3]

CHANGING ATTITUDES

Since that time and throughout history, people have felt both reverence and suspicion toward these furry felines. In Ancient Egypt, people thought highly of cats. There, if you killed a cat, you could be sentenced to death. Egyptians depicted Bastet, the goddess of love, with a human body and a cat head. Beni Hasan, an archaeological site on the eastern bank of the Nile River, south of Cairo, includes an ancient cemetery that contains the remains of 300,000 mummified cats.[4]

In contrast, in Europe during the Middle Ages (500–1500 CE), cats were seen as nuisances. They lived in dirty alleyways and were believed to carry germs. People associated them with witches and thought they were inhabited by the spirit of the devil. Villagers killed cats in droves to ward off evil. Some historians believe this may

CATS' CHINESE ANCESTORS

In 2016, researchers uncovered a possible strain of domestic cat different from those from the Fertile Crescent and Egypt. In China, local leopard cats had potentially been domesticated by farmers more than 5,000 years ago to help with the rodent population. The researchers studied bones found in an archaeological site in central China. One cat was buried in its entirety. "That's evidence of special treatment," said scientist Jean-Denis Vigne. "Even if what we're seeing here is not full domestication, it's an intensification of the relationship between cats and humans."[5]

have contributed to the spread of the plague, a disease that killed 40 to 60 percent of the European population in the Black Death pandemic of the 1300s.[6] With fewer cats to kill plague-carrying rats, the disease more easily spread to human populations.

In Dynasty 26 (664–525 BCE) of the Late Period, ancient Egyptians carved statues of the goddess Bastet.

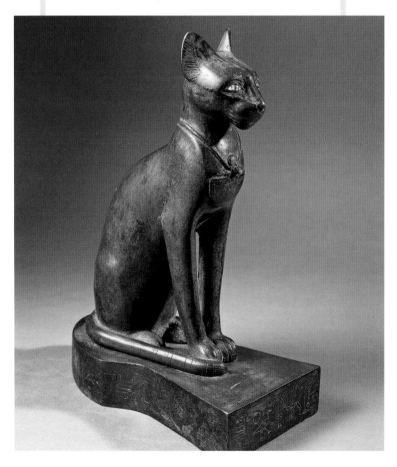

Though the domestic cat's DNA remains similar to that of *Felis silvestris lybica*, cats have small variations on specific genes based on the geographical area where their ancestors lived. In more recent history, cats have been singled out because of their appearance. Unlike dogs, which have been bred mainly for their hunting abilities or sense of smell, cats are now bred to carry on a specific coat color, texture, or pattern. Sometimes these cats compete in cat shows. One of the earliest cat shows took place in London, England, in 1871. Harrison Weir, known as the Father of the Cat Fancy, served as a judge and also wrote the breed standards. These standards specified how an ideal cat of a breed would look and act. Cats received awards based on their unique physical traits, such as the shininess of their coat, the length of their hair, or the color of their eyes.

TYPES OF CAT BREEDS

Cat organizations have different opinions about the number of cat breeds in the world. The International Cat Association recognizes 73 different breeds.[7] The Cat Fanciers' Association (CFA) recognizes 45.[8] Basepaws, a pet genetics organization, separates cat breeds into four main groups. Eastern cat breeds include Oriental shorthairs, Burmese, Birmans, and Peterbalds. Abyssinians, American shorthairs, Maine coons, Ragdolls, and Russian blues are all Western breeds. Persians, exotic shorthairs, and Himalayans are among the Persian breeds. Exotic cat breeds include Bengals and Savannahs.

Tama lived and worked at Wakayama Electric Railway's Kishi Station in Japan. After she died, she was named Honorary Eternal Stationmaster.

Today, cats are stars of the home and the internet. They are found in comic strips such as *Garfield* and star in social media feeds such as those of Grumpy Cat, Nala Cat, and Lil BUB. Some have even held positions of power. Officially designated the feline stationmaster in 2007, a calico named Tama prowled the platforms and station hallways of a train station in Japan's Wakayama prefecture. She waved her tail at passengers from her perch behind the glass window of her office, a converted ticket booth that housed her litter box and bed. She became so popular with commuters that she was promoted to Super Station Manager and knighted by the prefecture's governor. Tama died in 2015 at age 16. By that time, she had appeared in dozens of TV shows and captured headlines in magazines and newspapers across Japan and around the world. Thousands of mourners attended her funeral at the station.

Now Nitama, another calico, serves as the stationmaster. A cat named Yontama works five stations away. Both are on duty from 10:00 a.m. to 4:00 p.m., with two days off per week. The cats have "become very popular with people of all ages," says Keiko Yamaki, an executive for Ryobi, the company that owns the Wakayama Electric Railway. "We see lots of children and families and older people bringing their grandchildren. But also . . . couples and lots of overseas travelers come to ride the trains and see the stationmasters."[9]

CHAPTER 3

HOUSING
AND HEALTH

C ats can be relatively easy companions when it comes to care. As a species, they are mostly independent and don't need things like daily jogging or a trip to the backyard to go to the bathroom. Nor do they require a carefully regulated enclosure like fish or reptiles do.

But being a cat owner still includes some important responsibilities. In fact, one of the most important milestones in a cat's life comes at the beginning of its time in its new home. After deciding to adopt a cat, the biggest decision a pet owner faces is whether the cat will be an indoor-only pet, an outdoor-only pet, or a cat that sometimes lives inside and sometimes ventures outside for recreation or exploration.

People who want to get a cat should consider if they are willing and able to give a cat the care it needs.

INDOOR OR OUTDOOR?

Since the 1970s, the AVMA and much of the veterinary community have recommended keeping cats fully inside for many reasons. Indoor cats have less exposure to fleas and diseases such as rabies, feline leukemia virus (FeLV), feline immunodeficiency virus (FIV), or intestinal parasites than their outdoor counterparts. They aren't at risk of getting hit by a car or attacked by a wild animal or even another pet cat or dog. Indoor cats don't pose a threat

Owners of indoor cats need to make sure their cats get enough exercise and don't get bored.

to local wildlife either. Some studies show that indoor cats can live more than twice as long as their outdoor counterparts.[1] "Having your cat inside provides a safe environment for them and peace of mind for the owner," says veterinarian Dr. Kimberly Simmons.[2]

On the flip side, many experts say that an indoor-only lifestyle for a cat has its drawbacks too. A cat that lives fully outside or ventures outdoors from time to time benefits from participating in natural cat activities such as climbing trees, exploring nature, and hunting. Not only do these activities provide the cat with physical exercise and prevent them from clawing indoor furniture but they also give them plenty of mental stimulation.

Cats that go outside are constantly smelling the grass, listening to birds chirping, and feeling the wind on their faces as they scamper and play. As a result, they are less at risk of obesity, diabetes, and stress-related diseases, such as feline idiopathic cystitis. "Our felines have retained their wild streak. To see a cat outside is to see a creature in its element," says David Grimm, author of *Citizen Canine: Our Evolving Relationship with Cats and Dogs*.[3] To keep outdoor cats safe, experts recommend that outdoor cats be confined in a yard rather than allowed to roam, and many city laws require this.

Deciding whether to let a cat outside all the time, none of the time, or some of the time is up to each individual pet owner. Every situation is different—what's right for one cat or owner might not be right for another cat or owner. In any of those cases, pet owners can take plenty of steps to ensure their indoor or outdoor furry companion is living the best life it can possibly live.

CREATING A SAFE AND COMFORTABLE HOME

Whether they're living fully or partially indoors or outside full-time, it's crucial that cats have a safe and comfortable environment they can think of as home. For indoor-only cats, that can mean one room in a house or apartment that's fully theirs or an entire home where they can explore and run free. One of the most important requirements is a cozy, quiet place to rest that's out of the way of traffic, other animals, or bustling kids. Because cats spend about 70 percent of their lives

BARN CATS R US

Many people who choose to keep their pet cat outside do so for a specific reason—they've hired their cat as a resident mouser. In exchange for regular food, veterinary care, and shelter, the cat gets to do what it loves to do: hunt mice. Barn Cats R Us, an organization in King County, Washington, helps ownerless outdoor cats find homes in barns and garages throughout the area, where the cats work as rodent hunters. The program is free and is run by volunteers. All cats are checked by veterinarians to make sure they are disease-free before they are adopted and placed in new homes.

sleeping, a snuggly bed with sides to keep them protected and secure is a must-have in any home environment.[4]

For outdoor cats, providing a safe, secure, weather-protected structure for the cat to sleep in is mandatory. This can be a barn, an outdoor shed, or other enclosed structure on the property. Cats are susceptible to frostbite, hypothermia, and heatstroke just like humans are, so they need a place to go when the weather turns nasty. "A good outdoor cat house should have plenty of insulation and be waterproof," says Dr. Stephanie Ninnemann, a veterinarian at VCA Spring Creek Animal Hospital in Jackson Hole, Wyoming. "There should be plenty of room for the cat to stand and turn around but not too much room for them to get cold."[5]

Another idea for cat owners is to build or buy a specific structure for the outdoor cat to sleep in on a porch, balcony, or stoop if a barn or shed isn't available.

A COZY OUTSIDE SHELTER

Whether they're outdoor-only cats or indoor cats that sometimes like to sleep outside, felines need a safe place that will keep them warm and protected. The Kitty Tube Outdoor Cat House is made out of 100 percent recycled plastic, so it's weatherproof.[6] The inside, including the floor, is insulated with foam and comes with straw for comfortable, water-resistant bedding. The house also has an overhang to keep out rain and snow. The house can comfortably fit two adult cats or a female with kittens.

Heated cat houses are an option in places where the temperatures can dip below freezing. Most need to be connected to an electrical outlet and must be protected from the rain to prevent shock or electrocution. Other lower-tech choices are lined with insulating materials such as fleece, foam, or straw, which doesn't trap moisture

In shelters that house several cats, each cat has its own insulated cubby. Besides keeping cats warm, they also provide some safety from predators.

like cloth or wool. "In general, if it's too cold for you to be outside for any length of time, it is certainly too cold for them to be outside without proper shelter," says Ninnemann.[7]

Whatever the structure, outdoor cats need to have enough space to stretch out but not so much space that they feel vulnerable to predators. The structure should have just one door to limit the loss of heat in cool weather. If there are multiple cats, several doors or structures are preferable so the cats don't feel crowded or pushed to fight for space. If the budget is tight, some cat experts recommend building a simple outdoor shelter out of one 14-gallon (53 L) and one 20-gallon (76 L) plastic bin. The smaller bin is put inside the larger bin, with straw or Styrofoam insulation between them. "The big benefit of the bin outdoor shelter style is that it's waterproof," says Alley Cat Project volunteer Whitney Phillips. "It takes time and cost and muscle to put together, but it's easy to maintain, you just lift off the lid and stuff a bunch of new straw in."[8]

A TRIP TO THE VETERINARIAN

Once the housing situation is squared away, a trip to the vet's office is a must. Veterinary care helps maintain the cat's overall health and prevents it from spreading diseases to other animals. First, the AVMA recommends

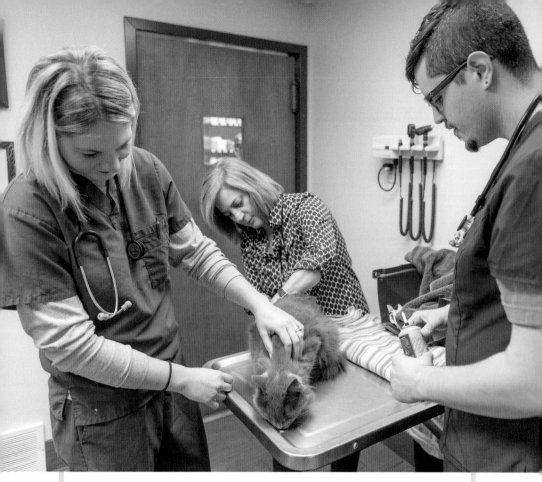

A trip to the veterinarian can be scary. Giving a cat treats during the visit can help make it a good experience.

that all cats, indoor or outdoor, should be vaccinated to protect them from several contagious or lethal illnesses. The AVMA's core vaccinations are for rabies, feline panleukopenia, feline viral rhinotracheitis, and feline calicivirus infection. These vaccinations usually last for a year, though some can last much longer or shorter. After the initial visit, most vets recommend annual wellness visits to make sure the cat remains healthy.

In addition to receiving vaccinations, all cats should be microchipped. This is a way to properly identify the cat in case it is lost or separated from its owners. The microchip is a tiny device about the size of a grain of rice. The vet implants the microchip under the cat's skin using a needle. The microchip contains an identification number that matches up with the owner's contact information in a database. If the cat gets lost, a scanner can be swiped over the chip to show the owner's name and location.

The third crucial thing a responsible owner should do to keep their cat healthy is to weigh the pros and cons of spaying or neutering to remove reproductive organs. Female cats are spayed, and male cats are neutered. The AVMA recommends cats be spayed or neutered by the time they are five months old. Most vets agree sterilization has a number of benefits, including preventing unwanted pregnancies and protecting against serious health problems such as uterine infections and breast cancer in females and enlarged prostate glands or testicular cancer in males. It can also eliminate the heat cycles in females, which can cause excessive yowling, and reduce the breeding instinct in males, which can cause spraying.

But there are also a few risks. Removing a cat's ovaries or testes also removes the hormones associated with those organs. This can lead to an increased risk of certain health issues, such as urinary incontinence. The AVMA

TIP FOR THE VET TRIP

Many cats associate their carriers with negative things, such as a ride in a loud car or a trip to the vet. But it's possible for a cat to link the carrier with more positive associations. Veterinarian Cheryl Yuill suggests teaching a cat to love its carrier by making it a safe space for the cat to spend time in during any day of the week. "Set it up as your cat's own private sleeping quarters or private dining room by placing their bed, food, and water dishes in the carrier. Or simply use the carrier as the spot where they get treats," she says. "This way, the cat can begin to associate it with the familiar sights and scents of home."[9]

recommends that pet owners ask their vet about the best course of action for their cat.

Whether it's to get spayed, to get vaccinated, or just for an annual checkup, a trip to the vet can be scary—especially when it involves riding in a car or other form of transportation. Cats are territorial and feel safest in their home environment. Anything outside that realm of routine can cause anxiety or fear. But cat owners can make the trip less stressful for their furry friends. Treats, toys, and blankets are important for the car ride to help the cat feel calm and surrounded by things it loves. Carriers, especially top-loaders, are also a must when taking a cat to the vet. They prevent the cat from escaping and also protect it from other critters that might be in the waiting room. "The most important criteria for a carrier: It should be easy to clean and you should be able to get your cat in and out

With a bit of training, cats can learn to feel safe in their carriers.

of it without a struggle," says veterinarian Tammy Hunter. "The ideal carrier is strong, lightweight, and waterproof, with a large opening to allow easy access to the cat, and an easy to remove top with 'quick release' fasteners. If you have a carrier with a removable top, your cat may be able to remain nestled in the bottom of the carrier while your veterinarian performs some parts of the routine physical examination."[10]

CHAPTER 4

FEEDING, GROOMING, AND PLAY

From feeding to grooming to playtime, taking proper care of a cat can be hard work. It can also be fun and very rewarding. The day-to-day responsibilities may feel a bit overwhelming at first, but the care becomes more manageable once it becomes a habit. "The joys of sharing your life with a cat are truly boundless," says Nina Kahn, a reporter for the website Bustle. "If you're considering taking the rewarding (but sometimes challenging!) plunge into cat parenthood, be smart about it and educate yourself on some of the difficult aspects of owning a cat that you might not be aware of now. Your kitty will thank you for it."[1]

Daily play is important for a cat's well-being.

MEETING CATS'
DIETARY REQUIREMENTS

Cats' ancestors lived in the desert. Because of this, their dietary needs are different from those of many other mammals. They require less water per day than a dog of similar size. Much of the liquid they ingest comes from their diet. This means it's important for cats to get enough moisture by eating the proper food. However, it's also important that cats have constant access to fresh, clean water. Many cats prefer running water, so a cat water fountain might be a good purchase.

In the wild, cats are natural hunters. Though domestic cats do not rely on rodents or birds for their daily meals, they still have those hunting genes and dietary requirements. They need to eat food that has high amounts of protein, small amounts of fat, and an even smaller amount of carbohydrates. The food also needs to contain important nutrients, such as vitamins, minerals, fatty acids, and amino acids like taurine, to keep their organs healthy and ensure their digestive system functions properly. Depending on their age and living situation, cats can be fed food geared toward their specific stage of life. Foods are made for kittens, adult cats, senior cats, and even indoor or overweight cats. Foods are also made for cats with health conditions such as sensitive stomachs or kidney disease.

Commercial food for cats comes in three main forms—dry, semi-moist, and canned. Depending on the brand of dry food, the ingredients may include poultry or poultry by-products, fish, meat or meat by-products, grains, milk, fiber, and various vitamins and minerals. Sometimes flavors are added to make the kibble more appealing to picky felines. Dry food is the least expensive type of cat food. It also contains the least amount of water, at 6 to 10 percent.[2] Though it will eventually spoil, the benefit of feeding a cat dry food is that it can be left out for grazing throughout the day. Moist foods cannot be kept out all day because they spoil quickly.

Semi-moist cat food contains about 35 percent water and is middle-range in terms of price. It's made of meat

HOW TO READ NUTRITION LABELS ON CAT FOOD

The best way to figure out if cat food is healthy is to read the label. Commercial cat food is produced based on the minimum nutritional requirements established by the Feline Nutrition Expert (FNE) Subcommittee of the Association of American Feed Control Officials (AAFCO). All pet foods that feature an AAFCO seal of approval are considered to be nutritionally complete and balanced. Similar to the labels on human foods, ingredients in cat foods are listed in order of decreasing proportional weight. The healthiest types are the ones that list meat, poultry, meat and poultry by-products, and seafood first or close to first. These foods have the most amino acids and fatty acids from animal sources. A veterinarian can also make food recommendations.

or meat by-products, grains or soybean meal, and some preservatives to keep the food fresh. Canned wet food is the most expensive but also the most beneficial for cats to consume. It contains at least 75 percent moisture and comes in a variety of textures, such as pâté, shredded, or chunks. Wet food is made of a variety of ingredients, including meat, seafood, kidney, liver, and even peas and pumpkin.[3] "The largest benefit of feeding a canned

Stainless steel is a popular choice for pet bowls because compared to plastic or ceramic, it doesn't scratch or break easily, bacteria don't grow well on it, and it is easy to clean.

diet is the higher water content. Cats with certain health conditions that require a higher-than-normal water intake, such as kidney disease, diabetes, or lower urinary tract disease, may benefit from the additional water in these diets," says veterinarian Cathy Meeks. "Canned food is also highly palatable, and some cats will eat a canned diet over a dry diet, particularly if they are picky eaters."[4]

Deciding whether to feed a cat dry food, wet food, or a combination can be a tough decision—especially if the cat is a choosy eater. Experts suggest that experimenting with flavors and styles to see what the cat likes best is the quickest way to ensure they maintain a balanced, healthy diet. If the cat will eat only dry food, owners could try adding a small amount of water to the kibble to increase its moisture content. If the cat hates pâté, owners could try shredded or chunked canned commercial food instead. Whatever the case may be, patience and a willingness to try new options are necessary when creating a suitable diet for a cat. "Every cat is different, and the amount you feed a day will depend on the age of your cat, your cat's current body condition, and the presence of any underlying diseases," says Meeks.[5]

Besides these forms, gently cooked and raw diets are becoming increasingly popular for cats. These diets can be bought from pet stores or made at home. It can be easy to miss nutrients in a homemade diet. Pet owners can work with veterinary nutritionists to ensure a pet is getting the nutrients it needs.

Lastly, a cat's diet wouldn't be complete without the occasional treat to put a pep in its step and brighten its day. The Cornell University College of Veterinary Medicine recommends keeping treats to between 10 and 15 percent of a cat's daily caloric intake.[6] Though some brands are more healthful than others, cat treats are generally not considered nutritionally balanced enough to be used as a dietary staple.

GROOMING AND CLEANING

Out of all types of pets, cats are considered one of the cleanest. They groom themselves constantly to get rid of soil and dust and to help cool down. Cat behavior consultant Beth Adelman says, "Grooming includes anything like licking, scratching or nibbling. They also shake and sneeze to clear their nasal passages, which some consider grooming as well."[7] But just because a cat is a natural groomer doesn't mean it doesn't need additional help from a human.

Cats benefit from regular brushing, especially if they have a lot of fur. This keeps their coats unmatted, removes dirt, and distributes healthy oils throughout their skin and fur. It also cuts down on shedding and hairballs, which can get caught in a cat's throat and cause coughing

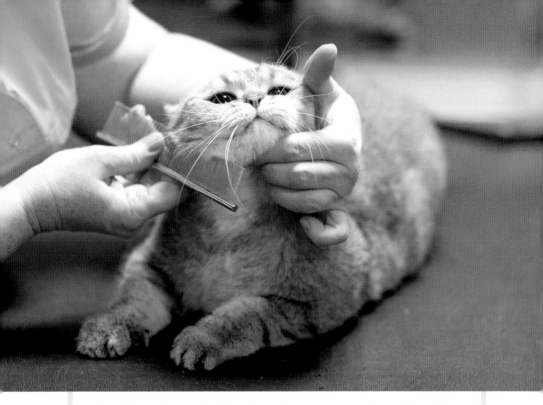

Metal combs and rubber brushes remove a lot of dead fur while doing less damage to the coat than a slicker brush.

or wheezing. A metal comb can be used to remove tangles and loosen dead fur. A rubber brush or one with bristles can be used to whisk the fur away. While shorthaired cats need to be brushed only once a week, longhairs can benefit from a combing routine a few times a week. Many cats don't like to be brushed around the belly, tail, or face, so cat owners should be especially careful in those areas.

It's important to make sure a cat's nails are routinely filed or cut. Overgrown nails can eventually curve, which prevents them from retracting completely.

Severely overgrown nails can grow into the cat's footpad, causing long-term pain and mobility issues. For this reason, most vets recommend cutting a cat's nails at least once every two weeks.

When trimming by hand, many pet owners wrap their cat in a towel to help it feel safe and protect themselves from unwanted scratches. They also use a clipper specifically made for cats, not humans. "Scissor-type

Owners should use only toothpaste made for cats. Human toothpaste is toxic to cats.

clippers . . . work great for clipping cat nails," says veterinarian JoAnna Pendergrass. "Guillotine clippers . . . also work well."[8] If all else fails, a vet or professional cat groomer can help with the nails and any other grooming needs, including ear cleaning and baths. Many cats develop dental disease even at a fairly young age. Regular teeth brushing and veterinary cleanings are important for a cat's health and comfort.

Finally, cats need a place to go to the bathroom, whether it's an indoor box or somewhere outside. The American Animal Hospital Association (AAHA) recommends that indoor cats should use a litter box at least 1.5 times their size.[9] The box should be placed in a quiet, out-of-the-way location where the cat feels most comfortable. In a multilevel home, one box per floor is recommended. If there is more than one cat in a home, there should be one litter box for each cat, plus one additional box. Litter boxes should be scooped at least once a day to keep the inside clean, sanitary, and odorless. Then they should be topped off with fresh litter. For nonclumping litter, the litter should be changed once or twice a week. For clumping litter, once every two weeks is fine.

Changing the litter and keeping the box clean will help the cat stay healthy and happy. Otherwise, accidents can happen. "If you notice your cat scratching outside

SELF-CLEANING LITTER BOXES

Cleaning the litter box can be unpleasant. It's full of germs, and it smells. There's an invention that can help with that problem: a self-cleaning litter box. Self-cleaning litter boxes like Litter-Robot work automatically. The litter is in a globe with a hole in the side. It sits on top of a lower compartment. After the cat uses the bathroom in the globe, a timer starts so the litter can properly clump. Then the globe slowly rotates. The clean litter falls through a grate, but the clumps stay above the grate. They drop into a compartment below. The globe rotates back to its original position, and the clean litter slides back into place. The chamber below the box, where the clumps go, has a carbon filter to prevent odors from escaping. The dirty litter can be removed from the bottom drawer and thrown away.

the litter box instead of inside, . . . it's his way of telling you that the litter box is disgusting and he doesn't want to get his feet filthy while he's 'attempting' to cover up his poop inside," says veterinarian Justine A. Lee.[10]

RELAXATION TIME!

Almost all cats love to do two things—nap and play. Each should be encouraged at home whenever possible. Thanks to the explosion of cat-related companies in the marketplace, cat owners have many types of beds to choose from. Some are soft, fuzzy, and flat. Others are multi-tiered nap-and-play towers with platforms to climb on, ropes to scratch, and padded or carpeted dens for sleeping. Because cats love to bask in the sun, many prefer a cat bed that's placed by a window.

Some owners hang cat hammocks from windows to give their cats a sunny napping spot.

When they're done napping, cats may jump, scamper, and play. Play is a way to satisfy a cat's need to hunt. Many like to bat around squeaky or squishy cat toys, including felted or feathered mice, small balls with bells inside, tiny stuffed animals covered in catnip, or a plastic bottle cap. Some cats will even play fetch. Others can spend hours chasing ribbon wands, searching out treats in puzzle feeders, or batting around crumpled-up paper in a cardboard box. Supervision is needed for toys that can be swallowed, such as ribbons or strings. Many cat owners have also trained their cats to do tricks using a clicker and a handful of treats as a reward. Giving an indoor cat at

PORTLAND'S ANNUAL CATIO TOUR

Portland, Oregon, is a city full of cat lovers. It hosts an annual tour of all the biggest, most creative, and downright fun catios in the area. It began as part of the Cats Safe at Home Campaign, sponsored by Portland Audubon and the Feral Cat Coalition of Oregon. This campaign seeks to reduce the number of cats living outdoors in the Portland metropolitan area by providing safe and beautiful environments in which they can live. One of the most amazing enclosures of 2021 was a Japanese-style, garage-sized catio made from bamboo, wire screens, and wood. The inside had part of a tree a cat could climb on, a cushy cat bed, and plenty of toys and platforms.

least an hour of playtime daily is essential to help prevent conditions such as urinary diseases or obesity, which can lead to diabetes. "Constructive playtime for a cat is much-needed exercise," says Dr. Carol Osborne. "One hour of play increases a cat's healthy lifespan by four hours. It often improves cats' mental health, too, lessening anxiety and destructive behavior."[11]

For indoor cats, spending time outside on a cat harness and leash gives them safe opportunities to explore. Indoor and outdoor cats alike benefit from an outdoor enclosure in which they can play freely. One option is to build a free-standing outdoor fence made of mesh that allows cats to see everything around them but also stay protected from other critters. Some pet owners who already have a fence in their yard build a fence-conversion

It is important to always walk a cat on a harness and not a collar because cats can slip out of collars or choke themselves if they panic.

system, which is a mesh or wire topper that angles inward and prevents the cat from jumping over the fence. Other owners build a catio, which is a patio designed for cats. Many catios are made of wood and mesh, have lots of platforms and resting places for cats to perch on, and are full of toys for playtime. "Learning what gets them excited, fulfilled, what provides them with joy, fun and enrichment is a wonderful experience for both the parent and cat," says animal behaviorist Russell Hartstein.[12]

CHAPTER 5

THE CAT
COMMUNITY

C ats are beloved all over the world. Multimillion-dollar industries have blossomed around not only their care and feeding needs but also their celebrity status. People read and write articles about cats, post TikTok videos about their cats, and even attend live shows where cats perform tricks.

But owning a cat isn't all fun and games. Becoming a responsible cat caretaker means understanding the costs involved and learning all about what being a cat parent might entail. This knowledge includes what happens during a vet visit, where to buy food and supplies, and what brands are the most trustworthy. People interested in owning cats often volunteer with or reach out to cat-centric organizations to learn what to expect over the course of their pet's life.

The Amazing Acro-Cats is one live cat performance show.

THE COST OF CAT OWNERSHIP

Depending on a cat's breed and where it lives, the average cost of owning a cat can vary. For example, a May 2022 study done by *Daily Paws* showed that a cat owner could expect to pay anywhere between $4,250 and $31,200 over the course of a cat's lifetime. That breaks down to between $425 and $3,120 on average annually.[1]

The first year of owning a cat is the most expensive. The price of adopting a cat usually falls between $30 and $180 at a local shelter but can cost $1,000 or more if the cat is purchased from a breeder.[2] Some breeds are more expensive than others. A Persian's price ranges from $500 to $5,500. A Bengal runs from $1,000 to $25,000, and a Savannah is from $1,500 to $50,000.[3]

An adoption fee at a shelter or rescue usually includes medical screenings, required vaccines, spaying or neutering, and microchipping. If any of those costs aren't included and need to be done at a vet's office, the costs can reach several hundred dollars, including the pet exam visit. Sometimes adoption centers or shelters reduce the price or waive adoption fees for low-income families or at certain times of the year if the shelter is overcrowded or they're running a special event.

After the initial costs, owners have other financial commitments to consider on a yearly basis. According to Rover.com, most cat parents spend between $150

Whether buying from a breeder or animal shelter, the initial cost of a cat is typically just a fraction of what the cat will cost over its lifetime.

and $750 each year on food, depending on the brand and type. Litter costs between $70 and $500 per year. Routine vet visits for a healthy cat can be $80 to more than $120 per visit if the vet is located in a more expensive area.[4] Typically vet care in cities costs more than vet care in rural areas. Of course, owning an animal also comes with emergencies or unplanned costs. These can include annual pet insurance, emergency vet bills, a one-time pet deposit for an apartment, grooming, and cat sitters or boarding. Additional costs include toys and cat furniture.

FOOD AND SUPPLY INDUSTRY

More than 370 million domestic cats live in the world.[5] To meet the demand, an entire industry is centered on providing them with everything they need. A handful of large corporations produce the bulk of the dry, semi-moist, and wet food for cats. Mars Petcare is the top global supplier, taking in $19 billion in annual revenue. It makes 28 brands of pet food for cats, dogs, horses, fish, and birds, including Whiskas and Iams. Nestlé Purina is the second-biggest supplier, earning $16.5 billion a year. It makes cat and dog food and treats as well as cat litter.[6] Its cat food brands include Friskies and Fancy Feast. Other major players include Hill's Pet Nutrition, J.M. Smucker, and General Mills. In addition to the larger companies, many medium-sized and small specialized companies also create treats and different types of pet food.

In the United States, pet stores and other businesses sell almost everything a cat needs. Cat owners can buy

FANCY STUFF FOR CATS

Cat supplies are sometimes criticized by cat owners for being ugly. "The problem is that cat scratchers and posts, while truly essential to your cat's happiness and well-being, have typically fallen into the 'ugh' decor category," writes Vetstreet reporter Caroline Golon.[7] But Jackson Cunningham decided to solve that problem. Inspired by his cat Jiggity, Cunningham opened Tuft + Paw in 2016. The company works with top cat behaviorists, engineers, and designers to create beautiful furniture for cats. So far, it has created a cat hammock made out of cozy wool, a folding cat tent, and plenty of comfortable beds, scratching perches, toys, and more.

food, treats, toys, beds, blankets, and litter at major pet store chains such as PetSmart, Petco, Pet Depot, Mud Bay, and Petland. Many smaller chains and locally owned pet stores also provide this service. If in-store shopping is difficult, customers can order through online retailers such as Chewy, Fuzzy, or the upscale Tuft + Paw. Supermarkets and drugstores often stock popular food brands in addition to carrying things like litter and toys. Large retailers like Costco and Amazon also sell cat food, toys, and treats in bulk.

Pet stores often have a wide selection of cat products, such as several kinds of furniture, to fit each cat's needs and preferences.

POPULAR PUBLICATIONS

For cat owners looking for more information, plenty of publications are available. *Catster* is the top-selling cat-themed magazine in the United States. Originally titled *Cat Fancy*, it publishes articles and tips about cat behavior, dietary needs, food, and health and wellness, as well as information about cat breeds and interviews with vets, breeders, and cat owners.

Modern Cat magazine is based in Vancouver in British Columbia, Canada. It highlights cat-themed do-it-yourself projects, cat food recipes, product reviews, and more. *Your Cat* is the United Kingdom's top-selling feline magazine. It runs helpful articles about cat adoption, rescue cats, kitten care, cat advice, and what owners can expect with certain cat breeds.

The *Journal of Feline Medicine and Surgery* (*JFMS*) is an academic publication. It's geared toward vets, researchers, and other people in cat-related professions who focus on feline medicine and surgery. *JFMS* publishes original papers, short articles, and doctoral case studies. It also features articles and guidelines about subjects such as illnesses and medical care, the latest surgery methods, and nutrition. It is an international, peer-reviewed journal and an official journal of both the International Society of Feline Medicine (ISFM) and the American Association of Feline Practitioners.

CAT-CENTRIC ORGANIZATIONS

Cat charities and organizations work around the world. Some focus on advocacy and outreach. Others promote change through education or legislation. Whatever their methods may be, these groups are devoted to improving the welfare of domestic cats worldwide.

EveryCat Health Foundation was established in 1968 by the Cat Fanciers' Association (CFA). Globally, it is the largest source of nonprofit funding for cat-related research grants. The foundation has given more than $8 million in funding to more than 200 cat health studies.[8] It also helped come up with a rapid test for vet clinics to test for feline leukemia virus (FeLV).

International Cat Care is a global charity established as the Feline Advisory Bureau in 1958 by Joan Judd and a group of cat lovers.

SENIOR CAT ACTION NETWORK

Many people agree that adopting a cat can be a rewarding experience. But sometimes older cats aren't given much consideration. That's why Veronica Iocona started the Senior Cat Action Network in 2020 after her elderly cat, Zoey, died. The charity focuses on cats ages 15 and up. It has a robust foster network where potential cat parents can take home an older feline. It also works with rescue centers nationwide to fund the medical costs of senior cats to give them the best chance of getting adopted. "Our goal is to give these cats every opportunity to find love again and remain safe for whatever time remains for them," its website says.[9]

They were discouraged by the lack of information available regarding cat health and welfare. The veterinary division of International Cat Care, the ISFM, works with veterinary professionals around the world to provide resources on all aspects of cat health. It also serves as a hub for cat parents looking for more information on how to take care of their pets. The charity has accredited more than 2,000 cat-friendly clinics in 31 countries. It also has more than 4,100 additional veterinary members in 109 countries.[10]

PetSmart Charities is an organization founded in 1994 by Jim and Janice Dougherty, the couple who founded the PetSmart retail brand. The charity helps make spaying and neutering services more affordable to low-income people. The leading funder of animal welfare in North America, PetSmart Charities works with nearly 4,000 nonprofit organizations and government groups, improving life for cats in Canada and the United States.[11]

Organizations like the CFA in the United States, the Governing Council of the Cat Fancy in the United Kingdom, and the International Cat Association put on hundreds of different kinds of cat shows each year where cats can compete for ribbons and prizes. The CFA works to educate people about cat ownership and promotes fair legislation surrounding feline welfare. It also sets the standards for every cat breed. The CFA International Cat

Show cats must be comfortable being handled a lot. The judge feels the cat and encourages it to move around so they can evaluate it against its breed standard.

Show is a competition among hundreds of cats that takes place in a different global city every year. The judges compare these cats to their breed standard. The closer a competing cat meets its standard, the better it scores. During the 2021–2022 season, the Best Cat and Best of Breed award went to a female long-haired Japanese bobtail. The runner-up went to a male white Persian. A female white Persian took home the third-place ribbon.

THE AMAZING ACRO-CATS

Many cats stand out on the internet. But some cats perform live and on stage. Founded by cat lover and trainer Samantha Martin, the Amazing Acro-Cats are a troupe of rescue cats that perform tricks and play music in front of a live audience. They can ride skateboards and jump through hoops. Some of the cats are trained to swipe at guitar strings or punch keys on a small piano. The hour-long act raises money for Martin's Rock Cat Rescue, a foster and adoption charity. The Amazing Acro-Cats have appeared on Netflix's *Cat People*, on Animal Planet, and on the *Late Show with Stephen Colbert*.

CAT SUPERSTARS

Some lucky felines win top prizes at cat shows around the world. Their fame is known far and wide within the show community. Other cats are internet sensations. They can become famous because of their looks, quirky habits, or ability to manipulate their humans.

Grumpy Cat was one of the original internet cat celebrities. Because of her underbite and feline dwarfism diagnosis, she always appeared to be frowning. Her owner posted countless memes with her face behind the punch line. Though she died in 2019, Grumpy Cat still had more than 2.6 million followers on Instagram in 2022.[12]

Honey Bee is a blind cat that was adopted from Fiji. She made waves when she starred in a YouTube video hiking the trails of Seattle, Washington, with her owners. Though she often rides on their shoulders, she also likes to walk wearing a harness and a leash to do some exploring. "You might expect a blind cat to be less able than a cat with eyes, but Honey Bee's boundless curiosity leads her to explore and enjoy everything the world has to offer," says Sabrina Ursin, one of her owners.[13]

Monty the cat was born without a nasal bridge because of a chromosomal abnormality. He lives in Copenhagen, Denmark. But people from all over the world follow him on social media. His owners, Mikala and Michael, adopted him from a shelter when he was three years old. Though he suffers from breathing issues and sneezes more than usual, Monty serves as an ambassador for "crooked cats everywhere," say his owners. "We also want to raise attention to the fact that looking different doesn't mean you can't be fantastic."[14]

Grumpy Cat's real name was Tardar Sauce.

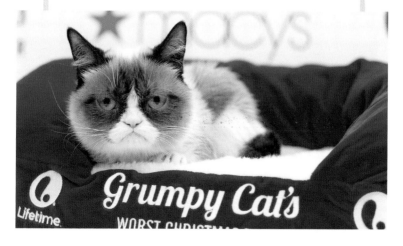

Some states don't have statewide provisions that specifically address cats, including Hawaii, Idaho, Kentucky, Ohio, and Washington. Only three states have comprehensive cat codes: California, Maine, and Rhode Island. Still, a few laws are common across states that apply to cats as well as other animals, such as animal cruelty laws, vaccination requirements, and laws governing the treatment of stray and feral cats.

COMPREHENSIVE CAT CODES

California, Maine, and Rhode Island are the only three states in the country with comprehensive cat laws. Each state provides full guidance on the ownership and sale of domestic cats within state borders. The laws in each state vary. For example, in California, all rescues and shelters must spay or neuter a cat before adopting it out, and they must provide proof of the surgery. At the end of 2018, California passed a law saying that pet stores could sell only cats from rescues or shelters. This prevented pet stores from selling cats from irresponsible breeders. Cats in California also fall under custody laws when a couple files for a divorce. A judge can assign sole or partial custody in court proceedings.

ANIMAL CRUELTY LAWS

Anti-cruelty laws exist in all 50 states and the District of Columbia, but they vary between states.[1] It is against the law everywhere in the United States to treat an animal cruelly, and that includes cats. In most cases, anti-cruelty laws prohibit the torture, mutilation, overworking, poisoning, or killing of cats in any situation.

In many of these states, it is also illegal to neglect a pet cat by not providing enough water, food, or protected living space for the animal. In Washington State, for example, pet owners may face misdemeanor charges if they fail to provide their cat with the proper shelter, sanitation, rest, or veterinary care. Abandonment of a cat or knowingly putting it in a situation that might result in bodily harm is also illegal in Washington.

If a person is convicted of breaking an anti-cruelty law, the punishment can range from a misdemeanor to a felony charge. Depending on the severity of the crime, punishments can include education and mandatory counseling, community service, payment of a fine, seizure of the animals, imposed limitations on owning any animals as pets in the future, and even jail time. In 2022, 49 states had laws that could lead to felony penalties for

SIGNS OF NEGLECT OR ABUSE

It can be difficult to determine whether a cat has been neglected or abused, but people can look out for some signs. Open wounds or many previously healed scars can be a sign of torture. Extreme thinness, a flea or tick infestation, matted fur or a dirty coat, and overgrown nails can be signs of neglect. However, these can also be signs of many other things. A cat may have escaped, been injured, and become matted and dirty but have loving owners searching for it. Either way, the cat should be assessed by a veterinarian or cat behavior expert to ensure appropriate treatment and care.

animal torture on the first offense.[2] Only Iowa did not. In California, a person can go to jail or prison for three years if convicted.[3]

VACCINATION-RELATED LAWS

In addition to anti-cruelty laws, the majority of US states have laws that deal with health-related issues to protect the health of both cats and humans. For example, many

Vaccines for cats typically work by injecting a weakened or killed virus or part of the virus so the immune system can learn how to fight off the virus in future exposures.

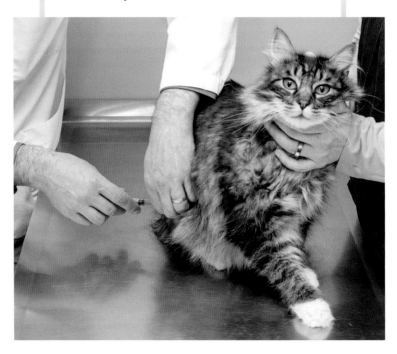

states require that cats be vaccinated against rabies before they are adopted out by a shelter or rescue. This virus often causes death in both animals and humans. For owners who take in a stray cat, it is their responsibility to make sure the cat has been vaccinated against rabies.

The age at which a cat must be vaccinated varies by state. In Mississippi, a cat must be vaccinated by a veterinarian by three months of age. In Kentucky or New York, the vaccination must happen by the time the cat is four months old. In Alabama, the cat must be vaccinated by three months of age and be vaccinated against rabies annually. In each of these cases, the owners of unvaccinated cats can be fined if they don't comply with the law.

FERAL CAT LAWS

Unlike anti-cruelty laws and vaccination laws, most states do not have any laws governing the ownership or care of feral cats. In fact, only 14 states and the District of Columbia have any laws that even mention the words *feral cats* in the legislation.[4] These states are California, Connecticut, Delaware, Illinois, Indiana, Kentucky, Maine, Nebraska, New York, Rhode Island, Texas, Utah, Virginia, and Vermont. Even in these states, the laws concerning feral cats are vague at best. Most of them leave the governance to local municipalities.

CATS IN TURKEY

In 2016, a documentary by Ceyda Torun called *Kedi*, which means "cat" in Turkish, was released to critical acclaim around the world. The movie follows seven stray cats as they slink their way into homes and sit beneath dinner tables throughout Istanbul, Turkey's capital—a city of 15 million people where more than 125,000 cats roam free.[5] The movie highlights a culture that not only appreciates cats but also supports their freewheeling lifestyle.

Turkey's love of cats dates back centuries. In Islam, a major religion in Turkey, cats are considered to be ritually clean animals. In the Hadith, a collection of traditions containing sayings of the prophet Muhammad, there are many instances where cats are upheld as divine creatures or animals to be treated with kindness.

In major urban centers throughout Turkey, restaurant managers feed stray cats after the daily rush

Cats take refuge from the cold in the Aziz Mahmud Hudayi mosque.

is done. People and local governments build insulated cat houses for strays to live in. In 2016 Mustafa Efe, the imam of the Aziz Mahmud Hudayi mosque in Üsküdar, even allowed cats in his mosque during worship hours. He became a social media celebrity in the process. "In Islam, we have a compassionate religion," he said. "We are responsible for these living creatures, they are our friends who cannot talk."[6]

For example, in Connecticut, a person or organization that feeds or provides shelter for a community or feral cat is called a keeper. All keepers are required by law to register with local animal control officers so that the cat is not impounded. In addition, any feral or community cat must be trapped if possible so it can be vaccinated, spayed or neutered, and then released. This process is known as trap, neuter or spay, vaccinate, return (TNVR). In Virginia, feral cats are considered companion animals, which means their caregivers can be charged with abandonment if they don't provide the cats with adequate food and water, a clean and dry shelter, and proper treatment and veterinary care. In both cases, these laws can be difficult to enforce because of the reclusive nature of some feral cats.

INTERNATIONAL LAWS

As in the United States, other countries and local governments around the world also have laws to protect cats' health and well-being. In addition to laws that regulate the distribution of vaccines, treatment of strays, and prevention of animal cruelty, many countries have laws that regulate cats' behavior. In Longburn, New Zealand, roaming cats are required by law to wear three bells around their necks to alert nearby birds. In Switzerland, people who own a single indoor cat are required to let it outside or give it a window from which it can see another cat so it doesn't get lonely. Another option for Swiss cat owners is to get a second cat to keep the first one company.

Japan has a curfew for the public display of cats, such as in cat cafés. No cats are allowed to be exhibited after 8:00 p.m. In Iceland, cats are banned from roaming free in some places, while other towns have curfews. In April 2022, Akureyri, a town in northern Iceland with anywhere from 2,000 to 3,000 cats, prohibited cats from prowling around outside at night.[8] A neighboring town, Húsavík, banned cats from going outside altogether, day or night. People in both towns—and throughout the country—still argue about whether it's kind or inhumane to ban cats from roaming.

CAT DEBATES

Whether they're in the home or live mostly outside, cats of all breeds, shapes, and sizes can be sweet and snuggly. But their care can be tricky. Sometimes passionate cat lovers disagree on what is best for their pets. Ever since cats were domesticated, the choices people have made surrounding the care of their cats—and the way they've dealt with those that didn't have homes—have stirred up controversy. Today, three main issues affect cats and their owners or neighbors. These are feline abandonment and the community cat population, cat breeding and kitten mills, and declawing.

COMMUNITY CATS AND THEIR CARE

Domestic cats can be divided into three major categories—those that are personal pets, those that are cared for by animal rescue centers

Persians are one of the breeds commonly sold by kitten mills.

or shelters, and community cats. The third category, community cats, are unowned. They are usually sociable stray cats or those who have been abandoned by their owners. Community cats can also be feral, or unused to socializing with humans.

The United States has approximately 80 million stray and feral cats.[1] Most community cats live outside in colonies, under bridges, in the woods, or in construction sites. Some are fed by well-meaning people in the neighborhood. Others scavenge for food on their own.

Some people care for community cats on their own properties, while others travel to known community cat locations, such as on Staten Island in New York.

Many ornithologists see these cats as menaces to the local bird populations. Further complications arise when the cats get into noisy fights at all hours of the night, sneak into people's trash cans, or suffer from health-related issues such as malnutrition, infections, and hypothermia in the cold. When the cats reproduce and have kittens, the problem multiplies. "The cat overpopulation problem is huge, and we must come together to address it as a community," says Jan Pridgen, a community cat caretaker in Wake County, North Carolina. "Cat colonies are usually hidden until dusk or dawn, and people are usually unaware of how pervasive the problem is."[2]

Community cats are among the cats that end up in shelters. The Humane Society of the United States (HSUS) estimates that three to four million cats—community or owned—are taken to animal shelters every year. At least half of those cats are euthanized because of age, illness, injury, temperament, or lack of sufficient homes. While approximately 85 percent of owned cats are sterilized, the remaining 15 percent can have kittens that may or may not find homes. According to the HSUS, only 2 percent of community cats have been sterilized, so they are the main source of cat overpopulation. They give birth to about 80 percent of the kittens born each year.[3] Sometimes community cats have caretakers, but many of those people cannot afford to spay and neuter an entire

People trapping cats for TNVR cover the traps to help keep the cats calm.

cat population. "These amazing caretakers provide them with food, water, care, and do all of these things for them, but if they don't have the resources to get them spayed or neutered, [the cats] have more and more kittens, and it becomes an absolute explosion of cats in that area," says Dr. Jennifer Bledsoe-Nix, medical director for the Society for the Prevention of Cruelty to Animals (SPCA) of Wake County.[4]

The cat overpopulation issue is ongoing. But one solution many experts have rallied behind is the TNVR program. Community cats are trapped, spayed or neutered at a local vet or clinic, given rabies shots in most cases, and returned to the outdoor home where they were trapped. Feral cats are returned instead of adopted out because they are often cautious around people and fearful of being confined in a house. Sometimes it is less stressful for the cat to remain outdoors. TNVR helps prevent community cats from having more kittens and increasing the kitten population. A tip of one of the cat's ears is also clipped or the ear is tattooed so TNVR volunteers can tell in the future which cats they've already trapped and released.

The TNVR initiative began in the United Kingdom in the 1950s. By the 1990s, it had caught on in the United States when an organization called Alley Cat Allies brought the solution into

JACKSON GALAXY: CAT WHIZ AND TNVR EXPERT

Jackson Galaxy, star of the Animal Planet series *My Cat from Hell*, is a cat behaviorist and influencer who has helped educate thousands of cat owners on how to best take care of their cats. He publishes articles and blog posts on cat behavioral issues. He gives advice on how to prepare a cat for a vet visit. He even does remote house calls to help owners gain confidence, "catify" their homes, and be the best cat parents they can be. Galaxy is also a big proponent of TNVR. "Whether you call them family cats, house cats, feral cats, community cats, alley cats, it doesn't matter—they are our cats . . . and they deserve our love and protection. . . . [TNVR] . . . does save lives. It is important," he says.[5]

the mainstream. Today volunteers, activists, and other organizations around the United States and the world are working to get TNVR accepted by more people. "There's a lot of contention out there about the cat overpopulation issues and community cats and a lot of very strong feelings from a lot of people," says Dr. Graham Brayshaw, a veterinarian for the Animal Humane Society in Minnesota. In this state, some cities such as Brooklyn Park have an overpopulation of community cats. "They've even done studies looking at animals that have been trapped and euthanized, or trapped and relocated . . . even removing those cats doesn't control the issue. They just rebreed, repopulate and refill. So sterilization is actually the best and most humane way to help control and start to reduce the cat population."[6]

KITTEN MILLS VERSUS RESPONSIBLE BREEDERS

Owners can adopt a cat from many sources. Some people find a stray cat and bring it to the vet for an exam, vaccinations, and spaying or neutering before taking it home. They can adopt a cat from a local animal shelter or rescue. Or they can buy a cat from a pet store or breeder. Whatever choice a person makes is up to them. But prospective owners do have some issues to consider regarding their choice.

Many accredited breeders raise cats for sale. These breeders take great care in making sure their cats are fed, well-loved, and treated in a healthy, ethical manner. They generally breed purebred cats like Russian blues, Bengals, or Ragamuffins—felines whose ancestors are all of the same breeds or whose ancestry includes crossbreeding that is allowed in the breed standard. But there are also breeders and sellers who treat their cats poorly or are only

A responsible breeder makes sure the mother and kittens are kept clean and healthy.

BENGALS

The Bengal is a medium or large cat that is known for its distinctive coat. It has a base color in one of several shades of brown with brown and black spots called rosettes, which resemble the markings on a jaguar, leopard, or ocelot. Because of its unique appearance, a quality Bengal can cost upward of $25,000 when purchased from a breeder.[7] However, the average price is $2,000.[8]

Bengals got their start in 1963 when breeder Jean S. Mill crossed a domestic cat with an Asian leopard cat. The female leopard cat had a litter, and one kitten survived. Mill named her Kin-Kin, and she became the first Bengal.

Most Bengals have green, yellow, or gold eyes. Some have

glitter, a sparkle at the tips of the fur that becomes visible when the light catches it. Their hind legs are slightly longer than their front ones, which makes them fast runners and good climbers.

Though most Bengals don't like to be picked up, they are very loyal and playful. They also enjoy learning new behaviors, such as turning off light switches. Because of their ancestors' habit of going to the bathroom in water to hide their scent from predators, some Bengals can even learn to use the toilet.

in it for the money. These places have been nicknamed kitten mills because of their factorylike conditions.

In kitten mills, the living quarters can be cramped and unsanitary. Sometimes the cats aren't given proper medical attention or enough love and affection. As a result, the cats can be vulnerable to infections, physical abnormalities, mites and parasites, or health complications due to inbreeding. Cats from mills might grow to be highly restless or emotionally stunted too, resulting in aggressive, jumpy, or skittish behavior. They may hiss, scratch, or bite in circumstances that wouldn't normally produce such a reaction.

Some states are passing laws to address the kitten mill issue. In December 2022, New York governor Kathy Hochul signed a bill that made the sale of dogs, cats, and rabbits in pet stores illegal. Known as the Puppy Mill Pipeline Bill, it would also put a dent in the kitten mill population by cutting off a profitable market for suppliers. "The cute puppies, kittens, and bunnies in pet store windows mask a sad reality: these animals are products of horrific neglect. . . . Puppy, kitty, and bunny mills use and abuse animals to churn out pets for sale, which are often riddled with congenital diseases, that cost unsuspecting consumers hundreds or thousands of dollars in veterinary bills and incalculable emotional stress," said Assemblymember Linda B. Rosenthal.[9] The bill

CFA BREEDER CODE OF ETHICS

The CFA represents the world's largest registry of pedigreed, or purebred, cats. In order to be considered and approved by the CFA, a breeder must abide by the CFA's code of ethics and must meet certain requirements. They must make sure their kittens are at least 12 to 14 weeks old, have been immunized against infectious diseases, and have received proper veterinary care before they are sold.[10] The kittens and cats must be kept in a healthy environment and properly registered by litter and breed. The breeder must also promise to deal with any potential buyer in an honest manner and continue to provide them with education or advice about the cat's breed when necessary.

allows rescue cats to be shown at pet stores for fostering or adoption, but the store is not allowed to profit from any fees associated with a New Yorker finding a pet there.

In contrast to kitten mills, reputable breeders take great care in making sure their cats are well cared for, healthy, and primed for adoption into a new family. The CFA lists recommended minimum standards that buyers can reference when looking for a breeder. It provides tips on how to interview breeders and how to ask if their animals were screened for breed-specific genetic health issues. For example, the conditions at a CFA-approved cattery or breeder must be sanitary at all times, adequately heated or cooled when necessary, and structurally sound. The cats must be fed

A responsible breeder makes sure kittens have items to play with and sleep on.

healthy, contaminant-free food at least once a day and their bowls must be kept clean at all times. There should be no evidence of neglect or punishment of any sort. Buying a cat from a cattery or breeder can be a daunting experience. But owners can take several steps to make sure they are buying their cat from a reputable source.

Cats need training to learn what they should and shouldn't scratch.

DENOUNCING DECLAWING

In their natural state, cats have a tendency to scratch. They do it to stretch their paws and legs. It's also a way for them to file their own nails. When left on their own, outside cats scratch trees, wood deck posts, and many other surfaces. If they haven't been trained not to do so, indoor cats can scratch furniture, clothing, bedding, rugs, and drapes.

Some owners opt to declaw their cat to solve the scratching problem. This involves surgical amputation of all ten of the front toes at the last joint when the cat is under general anesthesia. Other pet parents do it because they're allergic to cat scratches and want to prevent future immune reactions. Still others do it because they've tried every possible solution to prevent scratching and nothing has worked. Rather than rehome the cat, which can be costly or traumatic, they've chosen declawing.

As a practice that is not necessary for the health of the cat, declawing raises some ethical questions and doesn't have a lot of support in the veterinary community. More than 40 countries, including Australia, Brazil, and the United Kingdom, have banned declawing. In 2020, the AVMA revised its stance on the issue. Though it now leaves the decision up to the vet and owner, it strongly discourages the practice and suggests nonsurgical alternatives whenever possible. Many vets and feline behavioral experts agree with that decision. "This traumatic amputation requires significant healing. It can take anywhere from weeks to months for a cat to fully recover from being declawed," says veterinarian Jo Myers. "In some cases, a cat carries permanent pain or injury as a result of the declaw. Larger, older cats experience significantly more trauma during the procedure, and healing time is much longer."[11]

Nikki Martinez, assistant executive director of the Hearts Alive Village rescue, also frowns upon declawing. "Some [people] argue that declawing reduces rehoming and euthanasia, which comes about because of such scratching," she says. "However, as we have seen firsthand in our rescue, it may actually *increase* the chances of behaviors such as aggression and biting, which ultimately lead to rehoming or euthanasia."[12]

Cat owners have several options to avoid declawing and prevent or reduce scratching. If the cat will wear them, owners can try soft plastic claw covers that are glued on but are not harmful to the animal. Scratching posts are crucial, especially ones that are tall enough so the cat can stretch up to scratch. Regular nail trimming at home or by

ANTI-SCRATCH? TRY TRAINING.

Cats love to scratch. Many vets, animal rescues, and breeders recommend training kittens as young as eight weeks old to not destroy furniture. Some people use double-stick tape on high-scratch areas. Others spray citrus scents that discourage cats from coming near. One of the most effective methods is to use a clicker, treats, and scratching posts. When a cat goes to scratch a forbidden object, the owner should move the cat to the scratcher. When the cat scratches the post, the owner should use the clicker, then give the cat a treat. This way, the cat learns to associate scratching the post with a reward. If the training goes according to plan, the cat will scratch the post more frequently than furniture.

It's important to know what scratching surface and position each cat prefers so owners can provide appropriate scratching places. Scratching options include cardboard or rope at vertical or horizontal angles.

a groomer is also key. Myers says, "The most important thing cat parents can do to ease conflict over their cat's need to scratch is get good at trimming front claws and do it often. Once that's accomplished, and you've provided some suitable scratching posts, you're all set to coexist."[13]

CHAPTER 8

THE CAT'S MEOW

S tudies have shown that people feel great attachment to their cats. In December 2021, the *International Journal of Environmental Research and Public Health* published the findings of a study regarding cat ownership. In a study of 1,800 people who took care of at least one cat on a daily basis, 52 percent of the people viewed their cat as a member of the family. Twenty-seven percent equated the experience of caring for the cat with having a child. Fourteen percent saw the cat as a pet, and 7 percent thought of the cat as a friend.[1] What's more, a 2019 study published in *Current Biology* found that the feeling is mutual. Though the cat might not show affection in the same way, a pet cat will seek out comfort from its owner and express love, gratitude, and devotion in return whenever possible.

> Numerous scientific studies show the benefits of cat ownership.

MENTAL AND EMOTIONAL NEEDS

Many people say they feel better because of the feline presence in their lives. Research has shown that just having a cat around can lower stress, foster positive relationships, and even benefit one's overall health. In one study, for example, scientists shadowed the lives of 4,435 people for 13 years.[2] Out of this group, the people who had a cat or multiple cats were less likely to die from a heart attack than the people who had never owned a cat, even after researchers accounted for things like high blood pressure, cholesterol, and smoking. "Pets are good for people," says journalist Holly Spanner. "They improve our physical and mental well-being and bring pleasure into our lives. A contented cat can help you become a contented owner."[3]

MUTUAL AFFECTION

In 2019, scientists replicated a study done during the 1970s to investigate the parent-infant bond. This time, they used 70 kittens and 38 adult felines and their owners. Each cat was placed in a room with its owner. The owner left for two minutes, then came back. Researchers studied the cats' responses throughout. In the end, about 64 percent of the cats acknowledged their owner's return before continuing on with what they had been doing. Researchers concluded that this behavior meant the cats were securely attached to their owners, similar to what's seen in human babies. Scientist Kristyn Vitale says, "It's important for owners to think about that. When they're in a stressful situation, how they're behaving can actually have a direct impact on their cats' behavior."[4]

In return, today's cat owners work to ensure cats' emotional needs are being met along with their physical needs. Some pet parents are taking their cats for regular walks using a pet stroller, a cat backpack, or a harness and a leash. This activates cats' minds and all of their senses in addition to giving them exercise. "A lot of cats love to go outside and smell things, see things and roll around in sand and grass and dirt," says animal behavior consultant Sherry Woodard. "The cat is thinking more. It's thinking about how to use its body and what things smell like. The cats are brighter and engaged."[5]

Other cat owners are setting up bird-watching stations in their homes to satisfy a cat's curiosity. Cat owner David Mizejewski recommends setting up a bird bath or a hummingbird feeder near a window, then putting a cat perch or hammock next to the window to give the cat a bird's-eye view of the action. "Your pet cat will

STROLLERS AREN'T JUST FOR BABIES

These days, plenty of cat owners have been spotted taking a walk around their neighborhood with their cat in tow. Cat strollers are designed to spark a cat's enjoyment while allowing it to feel secure and safe. Some can be folded up and stored. Others have zip pockets and cup holders to keep treats for cats and humans within easy reach. Many are water-resistant or come with rain covers so cats can stay dry in the event of a drizzle. Cat-friendly strollers can cost anywhere from $50 to more than $300.[6]

A catio can help cats safely get closer to nature than they otherwise could indoors.

have hours of viewing pleasure and the wildlife will be safe," he says. "An added benefit is that placing feeders and baths close to windows helps reduce bird window strikes, another significant source of bird mortality."[7]

NEW CAT-APPROVED TECHNOLOGY

Many experts agree that giving a cat its daily needs—including clean water, tasty food, and a cozy shelter—is essential to ensuring it lives a long, healthy, and happy life. Doing things like taking the cat for walks, engaging its curiosity, and keeping track of its emotional needs are also key to its well-being. Making sure a pet cat's needs are met is easier than ever, thanks to a slew of new cat-related toys and gadgets.

If a cat owner is going on vacation, a few products can help make the time away more manageable. Timed, automatic feeders can be programmed to distribute dry food at certain times of the day. This way, a cat will never go hungry if its owner isn't home for feeding time. Petcube is a camera that can be placed anywhere in the home. It monitors a pet's comings and goings to give the owner peace of mind. It also serves as a security camera. For owners looking for a step up, PetChatz is a combination remote pet monitor and treat releaser. It has an HD camera, an LCD display, a motion detector, and even a function that allows a trained pet to call its owner with the touch of a button.

For owners looking to give their cats a bit of creative exercise, iFetch is an automatic ball launcher. While it's mostly made for dogs, some frisky cats can get in on the fun too. Iokheira makes an interactive ball that changes

CAT APPS GALORE

From emotional well-being to health and entertainment, there are plenty of reasons to keep a cat occupied—especially when its owner isn't around. Apps can help with the process. Friskies Cat Fishing challenges a cat to catch fish by pawing at a phone screen. Cat Clicker Training helps owners train cats by using a digital clicker. When the cat does a behavior the owner wants, the owner can press the paw pad to make a click sound. With some initial training, this sound tells the cat it did something good and will get a treat.

colors and direction when the cat chases it. It includes a feather, a bell, and catnip to take the fun up a notch. DJ Decks is a cat scratcher shaped like a turntable. For fish-loving cats, wireless fish toys have motion sensors and a remote for activation. Just one click and the fish flips and flops to the puzzlement and joy of the cat.

In addition to all the fun and games, plenty of tech gadgets on the market help keep track of a cat's health. Several companies make litter box monitoring systems that sit under the litter box. When the cat steps into the box, the system observes and logs the cat's weight and bathroom habits to make sure everything is on track.

A food puzzle is one low-tech option to enrich a cat's life.

Many people enjoy a close bond with their pet cats.

BELOVED COMPANIONS

For many people, having a cat in the family is a recipe for a peaceful, happy existence. Of course, many challenges come with raising a feline. The ongoing cost of care can be a drain on the wallet. It takes time and energy to care for a cat properly. The emotional commitment is high—and feelings of loss can be devastating if something unexpectedly tragic happens.

But a lot of cat owners feel the sacrifice is worth it. Some, like *Garfield* cartoonist Jim Davis, admire cats for their bravery: "Way down deep, we're all motivated by the same urges," he said. "Cats have the courage to live by them."[8] Others, like singer Amy Lee, appreciate cats because of the comfort and companionship they bring. "I love my cats more than I love most people," she said.[9]

But most of all, cats are creatures with ample love to give. Take cat owner Kira M. Newman's word for it: "I will continue to gush to everyone I meet about how happy I am to have a cat in my life—and in my bed, on my dining table," she says. "What I lose in sleep I make up for in soft, furry love."[10]

OWNING A CAT

Cats descend from solitary animals, but they still need plenty of time and attention.

DIET: Cats need fresh food and water daily. Cats' ancestors were from the desert, and since water was scarce, they got most of their moisture from food. Feeding domestic cats a moist food can help ensure they get enough water.

SPACE: Cats can be a threat to local wildlife. Safe ways for a cat to explore the outdoors include walking on a harness and leash, roaming around a cat-proof fenced area, or frolicking in a catio.

ROUTINE CARE: There should be one litter box for each cat resident, plus one extra. The litter boxes should be cleaned frequently or the cats may not use them. Rabies vaccinations are required for cats in most states.

ENRICHMENT: Plenty of play and exercise are key for all domestic cats. This helps their minds and bodies stay healthy and strong. Training at an early age is a great way to help cats learn to refrain from scratching furniture and be less fearful when it comes to interaction with humans or other cats.

KEY BREEDS

- Bengals were originally bred by crossing a domestic cat with an Asian spotted leopard.
- The Maine coon cat is a large, long-haired cat with a muscular body and big, tufted ears.
- The Persian is a long-haired cat breed with a flat face. Its thick coat needs daily combing to prevent tangles.
- The Savannah is a domestic cat breed that's been crossed with a wild cat called a serval at some point in its ancestry.
- The Siamese is a breed of slim, blue-eyed, short-haired domestic cats of Asian origin. It has a light body and darker ears, paws, tail, and face.
- The sphynx is a hairless cat breed from Canada. It may need to wear sweaters to keep from getting cold.
- Russian blues are steel gray in color, curious but calm, affectionate but not clingy, and intelligent.
- Ragdolls have long fur and a pale body with darker markings on the face, ears, tail, and legs. They are gentle and sociable to their owners.

GLOSSARY

calico
A pattern of a cat's coat that is a mixture of white, black, and orange patches.

catnip
A strongly scented plant in the mint family that is attractive to many cats and makes them playful.

DNA
Deoxyribonucleic acid, the chemical that is the basis of genetics, through which various traits are passed from parent to child.

encroach
To intrude or trespass in an area.

euthanize
To purposely and humanely end the life of an animal.

felony
A crime more serious than a misdemeanor, usually punishable by imprisonment.

feral
Relating to animals that live in the wild and descend from escaped or released domestic animals.

hypothermia
The condition of having an unusually low body temperature.

meme
An image or video that appears all over the internet and has a certain, often funny, meaning.

misdemeanor
A crime with less serious penalties than those assessed for a felony.

neuter
To remove the reproductive organs of an animal, especially a male.

ornithologist
A scientist who studies birds.

reclusive
Tending to seek out solitude.

registry
An organization that keeps an official record book that lists individuals of a breed and their family trees.

reverence
A feeling of deep respect or honor.

spay
To remove the reproductive organs of a female animal.

susceptible
Likely to be influenced by a specific thing.

vermin
Wild animals that are considered by humans to be pests, such as rodents.

ADDITIONAL RESOURCES

SELECTED BIBLIOGRAPHY

Grimm, David. "Were Cats Domesticated More Than Once?" *Science*, 26 Jan. 2016, science.org. Accessed 28 Sept. 2022.

Jondle, Amanda. "How to Help Your Cat Adjust to a New Home." *Pet News Daily*, 30 Sept. 2022, petnewsdaily.com. Accessed 28 Sept. 2022.

Moss, Laura. "Should You Let Your Cat Outside?" *Treehugger*, 16 Feb. 2021, treehugger.com. Accessed 28 Sept. 2022.

FURTHER READINGS

Drimmer, Stephanie Warren. *Cat Breed Guide: A Complete Reference to Your Purr-fect Best Friend*. National Geographic, 2019.

Mills, Andrea. *Cats: Facts at Your Fingertips*. DK, 2020.

Pearson, Marie. *Essential Mammals*. Abdo, 2022.

ONLINE RESOURCES

To learn more about pet cats, please visit **abdobooklinks.com** or scan this QR code. These links are routinely monitored and updated to provide the most current information available.

MORE INFORMATION

For more information on this subject, contact or visit the following organizations:

Alley Cat Allies

7920 Norfolk Ave., Ste. 600
Bethesda, MD 20814
alleycat.org

Alley Cat Allies is the United States' leading proponent of the trap-neuter-vaccinate-return (TNVR) program.

American Veterinary Medical Association (AVMA)

1931 North Meacham Rd., Ste. 100
Schaumburg, IL 60173
avma.org

The AVMA represents more than 99,500 veterinarians in the United States. Its website is a resource for cat behavior and wellness.

The Cat Fanciers' Association (CFA)

260 East Main St.
Alliance, OH 44601
cfa.org

The Cat Fanciers' Association is a nonprofit organization founded in 1906. It hosts and sponsors hundreds of cat shows worldwide. The CFA also promotes the welfare of all cats through legislative advocacy, supports feline research, and assists breeders in their businesses.

SOURCE NOTES

CHAPTER 1. CITY CAT, COUNTRY CAT

1. Quincy Miller. "How Long Do Siamese Cats Live? (Average & Max Lifespan)." *Hepper*, 21 Sept. 2022, hepper.com. Accessed 25 Jan. 2023.

2. Matthew S. Schwartz. "All Right. Some Cats Do Fetch." *NPR*, 5 Apr. 2019, npr.org. Accessed 25 Jan. 2023.

3. "AVMA 2022 Pet Ownership and Demographic Sourcebook." *American Veterinary Medical Association*, 2022, ebusiness.avma.org. Accessed 25 Jan. 2023.

4. "Browse All Breeds." *International Cat Association*, 31 July 2018, tica.org. Accessed 25 Jan. 2023.

CHAPTER 2. THE HISTORY OF DOMESTIC CATS

1. "Wild Cat Species—With Images." *Wild Cats Magazine*, n.d., wildcatsmagazine.nl. Accessed 25 Jan. 2023.

2. "Cats of the World." *Discover Wildlife*, n.d., discoverwildlife.com. Accessed 25 Jan. 2023.

3. David Zax. "A Brief History of House Cats." *Smithsonian Magazine*, 30 June 2007, smithsonianmag.com. Accessed 25 Jan. 2023.

4. Zax, "Brief History of House Cats."

5. David Grimm. "Were Cats Domesticated More Than Once?" *Science*, 26 Jan. 2016, science.org. Accessed 25 Jan. 2023.

6. "Black Death." *Encyclopedia Britannica*, 18 Oct. 2022, britannica.com. Accessed 25 Jan. 2023.

7. "Browse All Breeds." *International Cat Association*, 31 July 2018, tica.org. Accessed 25 Jan. 2023.

8. "CFA Breeds." *Cat Fanciers' Association*, n.d., cfa.org. Accessed 25 Jan. 2023.

9. Rob Goss. "The Cat Who Saved a Japanese Rail Line." *BBC*, 22 May 2019, bbc.com. Accessed 25 Jan. 2023.

CHAPTER 3. HOUSING AND HEALTH

1. "Can an Indoor Cat Be a Part-Time Outdoor Cat?" *PetMD*, 27 June 2018, petmd.com. Accessed 25 Jan. 2023.

2. Madeline Kennedy and Sorin McKnight. "The Benefits of Letting Your Furry Feline Live Indoors, according to Vets." *Business Insider India*, 18 June 2022, businessinsider.in. Accessed 25 Jan. 2023.

3. Laura Moss. "Should You Let Your Cat Outside?" *Treehugger*, 16 Feb. 2021, treehugger.com Accessed 25 Jan. 2023.

4. "All about House Cats." *Purina*, n.d., purina.co.uk. Accessed 25 Jan. 2023.

5. Shoshi Parks. "The 6 Best Outdoor Cat Houses in 2023, Including Heated Houses for Winter." *Insider*, 17 Nov. 2022, insider.com. Accessed 25 Jan. 2023.

6. Parks, "Best Outdoor Cat Houses in 2023."

7. Parks, "Best Outdoor Cat Houses in 2023."

8. Parks, "Best Outdoor Cat Houses in 2023."

9. Avery Felman. "How to Make Vet Visits Less Scary for Cats." *Wildest*, 13 Dec. 2021, thewildest.com. Accessed 25 Jan. 2023.

10. Felman, "How to Make Vet Visits Less Scary for Cats."

CHAPTER 4. FEEDING, GROOMING, AND PLAY

1. Nina Kahn. "11 Difficult Things about Owning a Cat That No One Tells You About." *Bustle*, 30 Sept. 2018, bustle.com. Accessed 25 Jan. 2023.

2. Cathy Meeks. "Wet Cat Food vs. Dry Cat Food: Which Is Better?" *PetMD*, 19 Jan. 2021, petmd.com. Accessed 25 Jan. 2023.

3. "Feeding Your Cat." *Cornell University College of Veterinary Medicine*, July 2017, vet.cornell.edu. Accessed 25 Jan. 2023.

4. Meeks, "Wet Cat Food vs. Dry Cat Food."

5. Meeks, "Wet Cat Food vs. Dry Cat Food."

6. "Feeding Your Cat."

7. "9 Things You Didn't Know about Your Cat's Grooming Habits." *BeChewy*, 20 Jan. 2021, be.chewy.com. Accessed 25 Jan. 2023.

8. JoAnna Pendergrass. "How Often Should You Trim a Cat's Nails?" *PetMD*, 6 Dec. 2018, petmd.com. Accessed 25 Jan. 2023.

9. "Keeping Odor Away with a Clean Litter Box." *PetMD*, 1 June 2020, petmd.com. Accessed 25 Jan. 2023.

10. Justine A. Lee. "How Often Do I Really Need to Clean My Cat's Litter Box?" *Pet Health Network*, 21 Apr. 2015, pethealthnetwork.com. Accessed 25 Jan. 2023.

11. "How Long Should You Play with Your Cats Each Day?" *PetMD*, 7 Dec. 2018, petmd.com. Accessed 25 Jan. 2023.

12. "How Long Should You Play with Your Cats Each Day?"

CHAPTER 5. THE CAT COMMUNITY

1. Sierra Burgos. "What Are the True Costs of Owning a Cat?" *Daily Paws*, 5 May 2022, dailypaws.com. Accessed 25 Jan. 2023.

2. "The Cost of Cat Parenthood in 2022." *Dog People*, n.d., rover.com. Accessed 25 Jan. 2023.

3. Mallory Crusta. "How Much Does It Cost to Own a Cat in 2023." *Cats.com*, 31 Dec. 2022, cats.com. Accessed 25 Jan. 2023.

4. "The Cost of Cat Parenthood in 2022."

5. Taylor Covington. "Pet Ownership Statistics." *Zebra*, 5 Jan. 2023, thezebra.com. Accessed 25 Jan. 2023.

6. "Top Pet Food Companies Current Data." *PetfoodIndustry.com*, n.d., petfoodindustry.com. Accessed 25 Jan. 2023.

7. Caroline Colon. "Am I a Bad Pet Owner If I Don't Want Cat Furniture All over My House?" *Vetstreet*, 15 Feb. 2015, vetstreet.com. Accessed 25 Jan. 2023.

8. Carla Shaik. "9 Best Charities for Domestic Cats (Complete 2023 List)." *Impactful Ninja*, n.d., impactful.ninja. Accessed 25 Jan. 2023.

9. "Home: Senior Cat Action Network." *Senior Cat Action Network*, n.d., seniorcatnetwork.org. Accessed 25 Jan. 2023.

10. Shaik, "9 Best Charities for Domestic Cats."

11. Shaik, "9 Best Charities for Domestic Cats."

12. Grumpy Cat. "Realgrumpycat." *Instagram*, n.d., instagram.com. Accessed 25 Jan. 2023.

13. Hiker Cass. "Meet Honey Bee, the Blind Hiking Cat." *Washington Trails Association*, 14 Nov. 2014, wta.org. Accessed 25 Jan. 2023.

14. Dovas. "Meet Monty: The Adorable Cat with an Unusual Face." *Bored Panda*, 2015, boredpanda.com. Accessed 25 Jan. 2023.

CHAPTER 6. LAWS AND REGULATIONS

1. "Animal Cruelty Facts: Understanding the Law and the Link." *Alley Cat Allies*, n.d., alleycat.org. Accessed 25 Jan. 2023.

2. "Animal Cruelty Facts and Stats." *Humane Society of the United States*, n.d., humanesociety.org. Accessed 25 Jan. 2023.

3. "Penal Code 597 PC—California 'Animal Abuse' & Cruelty Laws." *Shouse California Law Group*, n.d., shouselaw.com. Accessed 25 Jan. 2023.

4. Laura Nirenberg. *Community Cats and the Law*. Best Friends Animal Society, n.d., humanesociety.org. Accessed 25 Jan. 2023.

5. Didem Tali. "A New Deal for Turkey's Homeless Dogs." *New York Times*, 2 Oct. 2019, nytimes.com. Accessed 25 Jan. 2023.

6. Kareem Shaheen. "Turkey: Where Pampered Cats Are Top Dog." *Guardian*, 28 Dec. 2017, theguardian.com. Accessed 25 Jan. 2023.

7. "Feral Cat Feeding Bans: The Reasoning, Risks, and Results." *National Feline Research Council*, n.d., felineresearch.org. Accessed 25 Jan. 2023.

8. Egill Bjarnason. "It's 10 PM. Do You Know Where Your Cat Is?" *Hakai Magazine*, 17 May 2022, hakaimagazine.com. Accessed 25 Jan. 2023.

CHAPTER 7. CAT DEBATES

1. "Why Activists Are Fighting over Feral Felines." *PBS NewsHour*, 22 Jan. 2016, pbs.org. Accessed 25 Jan. 2023.

2. "Volunteers and the SPCA of Wake County Are on a Mission to End Cat Suffering and Overpopulation in NC." *WRAL News*, 16 Dec. 2022, wral.com. Accessed 25 Jan. 2023.

3. *An Overview of Caring for Outdoor Cats*. Humane Society of the United States, n.d., humanesociety.org. Accessed 25 Jan. 2023.

4. "Volunteers and the SPCA of Wake County Are on a Mission."

5. "What Are 'Community Cats?' Jackson Galaxy Helped Me See." *Catster*, 16 Oct. 2014, catster.com. Accessed 25 Jan. 2023.

6. Heidi Wigdahl. "Animal Rescues Work with City to Address Cat Colonies in Brooklyn Park Neighborhood." *Kare11*, 7 Sept. 2022, kare11.com. Accessed 25 Jan. 2023.

7. Dean Eby. "Top 20 Most Expensive Cat Breeds in the World (with Pictures)." *PetKeen*, 18 Jan. 2023, petkeen.com. Accessed 25 Jan. 2023.

8. "Reserving a Bengal Kitten." *A-Kerr's Bengal Cats*, n.d., akerrsbengals.com. Accessed 25 Jan. 2023.

9. "New York Lawmakers Pass Groundbreaking Bill to End the Retail Sale of Dogs, Cats, and Rabbits in Pet Stores." *CISION PR Newswire*, 3 June 2022, prnewswire.com. Accessed 25 Jan. 2023.

10. "FAQs: How Do I Know a Breeder Is 'Reputable'?" *Cat Fanciers' Association*, n.d., find-a-breeder.cfa.org. Accessed 25 Jan. 2023.

11. Paige Cerulli. "Is It Bad to Declaw a Cat? This Is What the Experts Have to Say." *Pawtracks*, 17 Sept. 2022, pawtracks.com. Accessed 25 Jan. 2023.

12. Cerulli, "Is It Bad to Declaw a Cat?"

13. Cerulli, "Is It Bad to Declaw a Cat?"

CHAPTER 8. THE CAT'S MEOW

1. Esther M. C. Bouma, Marsha L. Reijgwart, and Arie Dijkstra. "Family Member, Best Friend, Child or 'Just' a Pet, Owners' Relationship Perceptions and Consequences for Their Cats." *International Journal of Environmental Research and Public Health*, vol. 19, no. 1, 24 Dec. 2021, pubmed.ncbi.nlm.nih.gov. Accessed 25 Jan. 2023.

2. Kira M. Newman. "The Science-Backed Benefits of Being a Cat Lover." *Healthline*, 22 Oct. 2019, healthline.com. Accessed 25 Jan. 2023.

3. Holly Spanner. "Best Cat Gadgets to Help Them Live a Life of Luxury." *BBC Science Focus*, 17 Feb. 2022, sciencefocus.com. Accessed 25 Jan. 2023.

4. Sarah Jackson. "Cats Really Do Need Their Humans, Even If They Don't Show It." *NBC News*, 23 Sept. 2019, nbcnews.com. Accessed 25 Jan. 2023.

5. Kate Bratskeir. "How to Walk Your Cat on a Leash, and Why You Should." *HuffPost*, 25 June 2015, huffpost.com. Accessed 25 Jan. 2023.

6. Karen Anderson and Zibby Wilder. "The Best Cat Strollers for Taking Your Cat Everywhere." *Dog People*, n.d., rover.com. Accessed 25 Jan. 2023.

7. David Mizejewski. "11 Tips to Keep Your Indoor Cat Happy." *National Wildlife Federation Blog*, 10 Nov. 2020, blog.nwf.org. Accessed 25 Jan. 2023.

8. Nicol Natale and Alesandra Dubin. "45 Adorable Cat Quotes That Will Melt Your Heart." *Woman's Day*, 28 Dec. 2021, womansday.com. Accessed 25 Jan. 2023.

9. Amy Lee. "25 Things You Don't Know about Me: Amy Lee." *Yahoo! Entertainment*, 11 Oct. 2011, yahoo.com. Accessed 25 Jan. 2023.

10. Newman, "Science-Backed Benefits of Being a Cat Lover."

Alexis Burling has written dozens of articles and books for young readers on a variety of topics ranging from current events and biographies of famous people to nutrition and fitness. She is also a professional book critic with reviews of adult and young adult books, author interviews, and other publishing industry–related articles in the *New York Times*, the *Washington Post Book World*, the *San Francisco Chronicle*, and more. Alexis lives in White Salmon, Washington, with her husband. She has had the privilege of loving and caring for four stupendous cats in her life: Brandy (a fierce stray–turned–house cat that slept in a cradle); Sam (a beloved tuxedo that loved snuggling and scratching furniture); and her two current cats, Suki (a blue point Siamese that loves to yip and fetch) and LB (an outdoor-only tabby with a propensity for head-bonking).